N. K. RUTTER

GREEK COINAGE

D1437666

SHIRE ARCHAEOLOGY

Cover photograph

Facing head of Apollo on a tetradrachm of Katane,
Sicily, *c* 405 BC.
(Photograph: Hunterian Museum.)

Maps by D. A. Darton. Fig. 2 drawn
by David J. Eveleigh.

Published by
SHIRE PUBLICATIONS LTD
Cromwell House, Church Street, Princes Risborough,
Aylesbury, Bucks, HP17 9AJ, UK.

Series Editor: James Dyer

Copyright © N. K. Rutter, 1983.
All rights reserved.
No part of this publication may be reproduced or transmitted in any form or by any means,
electronic or mechanical, including photocopy, recording, or any information storage and
retrieval system, without permission in writing from the publishers.

ISBN 0 85263 635 0

First published 1983

Set in 11 on 11 point Times roman and printed in Great Britain by C. I. Thomas & Sons
(Haverfordwest) Ltd, Press Buildings, Merlins Bridge, Haverfordwest.

Contents

4

List of illustrations

The coins illustrated in plates 1-15 are all reproduced actual size.

Preface

Most of the technical terms used in this book are explained when they first appear in the text. Table 1 on page 32 explains the various permutations of drachms. The captions to the plates include a basic minimum of information: issuing authority and date, metal and denomination, brief descriptions of types. All dates are BC.

It is a particular pleasure to acknowledge the encouragement and advice of friends and colleagues in the preparation of the text and plates. The coins illustrated on plate 1, numbers 1-3, and on plate 8, numbers 1-10, are from the collection of the Ashmolean Museum, Oxford, and, in one case, from the British Museum, and I thank Dr Daphne Nash and Dr Martin Price for arranging for them to be photographed. All the other coins illustrated are from the Hunter Coin Cabinet, housed in the Hunterian Museum, University of Glasgow; references in the captions are to Sir George MacDonald's *Catalogue of Greek Coins in the Hunterian Collection* (three volumes), 1899-1905. My warmest thanks are due to Dr Donal Bateson, keeper of the Hunter Cabinet, for his unstinting help at every stage of this project.

In 1783 William Hunter bequeathed his cabinet of coins to the University of Glasgow. Hunter made his bequest because he believed that it would most likely lead to the use of his collection 'for the improvement of knowledge'. The following pages aim to make a modest contribution to the fulfilment of Hunter's wishes.

Department of Greek, University of Edinburgh

1
Introduction

The scope of Greek coinage is very wide, both geographically and chronologically. From 1000 onwards the Greek mainland was the base for several waves of emigration to many parts of the coasts of the Mediterranean and Black seas. In the west, Greeks settled in Spain and southern France and founded many prosperous cities in Sicily and southern Italy. In the east and north-east, the Aegean and Black seas were particularly thickly settled. In Libya, the city of Cyrene became a flourishing centre of Greek influence. In all these areas, when coins began to be issued, they were issued by Greek cities and for Greeks. Various neighbours of the Greeks, such as the Carthaginians in north Africa and Sicily, the Etruscans in Italy and the Persians in their provinces in western Asia, were deeply influenced by many of the material aspects of Greek culture, and among the practices they adopted from the Greeks, at various times, was that of minting coins. Such coins often bear images and inscriptions appropriate to the peoples by whom they were minted, but their general appearance was modelled on that of Greek coins, and they are usually included, in catalogues and other works, in the section devoted to Greek coins. A final large extension of the area of Greek coinage resulted from the campaigns of Alexander III of Macedon (Alexander the Great). By the time he died at Babylon in 323, his armies had helped to introduce elements of Greek culture to vast areas of what we now call the Middle East. After his death his generals fought over his inheritance, and several were to become kings in their own right, for example in Egypt, Syria and the Middle East, and Macedonia. Later still, other kingdoms were carved out of Alexander's legacy, for example those based on Pergamum, in north-western Anatolia, or Bactria, now divided between southern Russia and northern Afghanistan. The Greek rulers of most of the known kingdoms issued coins, as from time to time did many individual cities in their territories.

Thus Greek coinage is a very wide field of study, embracing most of the non-Roman coinage of the ancient world struck between the Straits of Gibraltar and north-west India. An introductory book must select, but its central concern must be the coins themselves, their visual impact and the images they present. To contemplate a collection of Greek coins is to contemplate the variety, and at the same time the essential unity, of the Greek world. But there is also much interest in technical matters such as the methods used to make coins, and in the question of how coins were used in the Greek world. The following pages aim to unite these three strands of interest: the nature of the coins themselves, the description of what is represented on them, and the problems of function and use. The first two chapters describe the beginning of coinage and outline the essential characteristics of a Greek coin. Chapter 3 presents a representative selection of coins from a self-contained area of the Greek world, the city-states of south Italy and Sicily, and chapter 4 discusses the use of coins in one city-state, Athens. Finally, chapter 5 presents coins of Philip II of Macedon, his son Alexander the Great, and their successors in the Hellenistic kingdoms.

2
The invention of coinage

Nowadays we are so used to making everyday purchases with coins that it is difficult to imagine how we could do without such an apparently necessary means of survival. Yet it was not always so: the production and use of coined money was a comparatively late development in the long history of exchanges made through the medium of a variety of objects and materials, including precious metals.

The ancient civilisations of Mesopotamia and Egypt, and of the Aegean basin too, provide examples of the use of metals as an article of trade or as a measure of value. Metals figure also among the variety of media of exchange referred to in cuneiform texts from Mesopotamia — barley, gold, lead and silver, the last most generally, and especially in later periods. When metal was used, it had to be weighed in a balance, against one of the recognised weight systems, which varied from time to time and from place to place. Weights from these, in stone and other materials, have been found. The word *shekel* is now commonly thought of as referring to a unit of coinage, but the root *šql* in Hebrew, like its counterpart in other Semitic languages, expresses the action of weighing. Some of the most accessible and illuminating references to the weighing out of uncoined metal for a variety of purposes are to be found in the Old Testament. For example, when Abraham bought a field, he weighed out the silver for the price (Genesis 23, 16), and contributions to a temple repair fund were first collected in a receptacle with a hole bored in its lid, then counted out by weight (2 Kings 12, 10 ff). Greek terminology too reflects this background: for example, the word *stater,* referring to the principal denomination of a coinage, derives from a root one of whose meanings is 'weigh'.

Metal weighed out thus to effect the exchange of goods and services is *currency*. Currency becomes *money* when the metal used in the exchange is made up in specific forms and according to specific weight standards. *Coinage* goes a step further than that: in addition to being prepared in units of standardised weight, the metal must be marked in some recognisable way with the stamp of an authority to guarantee its accurate weight and quality (or *fineness*). These characteristics of a true coinage have not so far been found together either in ancient Egypt or in the sophisticated economies of the early Mesopotamian kingdoms.

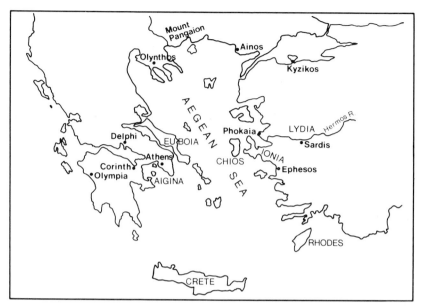

Fig. 1. Greece and western Asia Minor.

From a combination of literary evidence and archaeological discoveries it appears that the first western coinage was struck in quite a small area of central western Anatolia, namely the area of coast and hinterland watered by the lower reaches of the Hermos river. This area was the point of contact between Greek settlements, such as Ephesos, on the coast and the kingdom of Lydia occupying an intermediate position between sea coast and interior plateau, with its capital at the spectacular site of Sardis (fig. 1).

The Lydians, who first figure in history in the seventh century, were regarded by the historian Herodotus, writing in the fifth century, as the first users of coinage. One of the most famous streams of antiquity, the Pactolos, flowed just to the west of the acropolis of Sardis, before joining the Hermos, and it was probably from the ore found in its bed that the first coins were made. This ore was electrum, a natural alloy of gold and silver. Recent research, while confirming the western Anatolian origin of coinage, shows that the Greeks contributed much, if not to its invention, then certainly to its development from a very early stage. The most instructive evidence for the nature and dating of the first coins comes not from Lydian territory, but from the excavations of the temple of Artemis at Ephesos, published early in the twentieth century. Here a miscellaneous deposit of beads, pins, brooches and figurines, none of which can be dated later than the early years of the sixth century, contained also some of the earliest electrum coins. These exhibited varying degrees of elaboration, and it was possible to define a progression from small nuggets of metal to coins marked with a design, and to estimate the 'birth of coinage' as having taken place in the last quarter of the seventh century. Finally, the concept and technique of engraving the designs stamped on coins are closely allied to those of engraving seal stones, but in Anatolia seal engraving began only with the fall of king Croesus of Lydia about 546. The Greeks, on the other hand, had long been accustomed to the idea of engraving and using seals, and this contribution to the beginning of coinage was probably theirs. It was a common culture of Lydians and Greeks which produced, among other things, the first western coins.

The coins on plate 1 illustrate some of the early stages of coinage in Asia Minor and its diffusion to mainland Greece. Numbers 1 to 3 are electrum coins. The surface of the obverse of number 1 (for discussion of the terms obverse and reverse, see page 15 below) is marked with nothing more elaborate than a number of roughly parallel lines, or *striations;* its reverse has received the imprint of a simple punch. The obverse of number 2 bears an easily recognisable design, the foreparts of a lion and a bull back to back, which has been attributed to king Croesus, but still the reverse is marked only with punches.

From Lydia and Ionia the idea of coinage spread northwards to such cities as Kyzikos, and westwards across the Aegean, via islands such as Chios (plate 1, number 3). In mainland Greece the first cities to issue coins appear to have been Aigina and Corinth, around the middle of the sixth century. Their respective badges were a turtle and the winged horse Pegasus, seen here on the obverse of early coins with punched reverse (plate 1, numbers 4 and 5).

Why was coinage invented? No precise answer can be given to that question. Our own experience of coinage is in everyday

Plate 1. EARLY COINAGE
1. Ionia, electrum quarter-stater, 650-600. Obverse: striations. Reverse: punch. Oxford.
2. Lydia, electrum stater, 561-545. Obverse: foreparts of lion and bull. Reverse: punches. Oxford. **3.** Chios, electrum stater, *c* 550. Obverse: sphinx. Reverse: punch. Oxford.
4. Aigina, silver stater, *c* 500. Obverse: turtle. Reverse: punch. Hunter 1. **5.** Corinth, silver stater, 550-500. Obverse: Pegasus. Reverse: 'swastika' punch. Hunter 1.

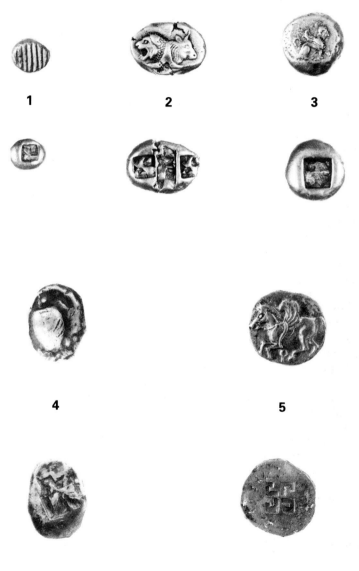

transactions of buying and selling, but it does not follow that this was its purpose from the beginning, and it is important not to exaggerate the economic significance of the new medium. It did not render obsolete the older methods of exchange. Even after coinage was invented, many Greek states and non-Greek peoples such as the Phoenicians, who were very active traders, managed satisfactorily for years without minting coins of their own. For large transactions coinage was not necessarily advantageous; as for small, everyday transactions, many states never issued the full range of those smaller coins that make possible ordinary buying and selling in a market.

What then were these early coins produced for? In later periods military events were frequently the occasion for Greek coinage — the preparation and operation of fleets and armies might require a large number of standardised payments for equipment and men, and after a campaign was over the victors often faced the problem of how to distribute most conveniently the proceeds of booty or indemnity. It has been suggested therefore that the very first coins may have been issued in response to military needs, more precisely for the payment of mercenary soldiers. The nature of some of these coins — their standardised weights and the obverse design of a lion's head — suggests that they were issued to make a large number of uniform and valuable payments in a portable and durable form, and that the authority or person making the payment was the king of Lydia. Not all the recipients of these pieces would wish to retain them. Many pieces might be exchanged for goods or services and would thus circulate as money. As we have seen, the new kind of currency was soon copied elsewhere, though possibly not always for the same reasons.

So the first coins were a stage in a process. These pieces of accurately weighed and stamped metal were not without antecedents, and the new combination of features provided the basis for developments many years, even centuries, in the future.

3
The character of Greek coinage

Once invented, coinage spread rapidly in a generally westward direction, from Asia Minor by way of the Aegean to mainland Greece, and thence to Italy and Sicily. The frequently crude and irregular shapes of the earliest coins quickly gave way to pieces that are more recognisably the precursors of modern coins, generally circular, and with designs on each side.

For almost two hundred years after their first appearance Greek coins were minted only from precious metals — first electrum, then silver or gold. Gold was scarce in the Greek world and tended to be used only for emergency coinages like that issued at Athens in the last decade of the fifth century, when the Athenians were cut off from their silver mines at Laurion (see chapter 5). Silver, though more common than gold, was still not very widely or plentifully distributed. Few cities commanded supplies in their own territories, and the majority depended on a variety of outside sources, which sometimes included the coins of other cities. The issue of coins requires not only the stimulus of a suitable occasion, but also a supply of metal to turn into coins. The comparative scarcity of precious metals helps to explain why not every city coined and why in others the issue of coins was irregular. Regular and prolific coin production by any one authority was not common until the age of Philip II of Macedon and his son Alexander III (the Great). Coins in precious metals had an intrinsic value as bullion, but the adoption of bronze as a metal for coinage in some parts of the Greek world (notably the north Aegean, Sicily and south Italy) during the fifth century introduced the idea of a token coinage, in which the intrinsic value of the metal in a coin is much less than the coin's value as a medium of exchange.

Ancient Greece was not a unified state — still less so the various parts of the Mediterranean and Black Sea coasts settled by Greeks. The variety of origin, traditions and customs of the Greek cities is reflected in the variety of their independent coinages, minted on different and often unrelated weight standards. For example, on the island of Aigina (and in much of mainland Greece and on some of the islands of the Aegean, including Crete), a drachm of silver weighed approximately 6 grams, and the *stater* was a didrachm. At Athens on the other hand, just across the water from Aigina, a different standard, the

Fig. 2. The Greek method of coining.

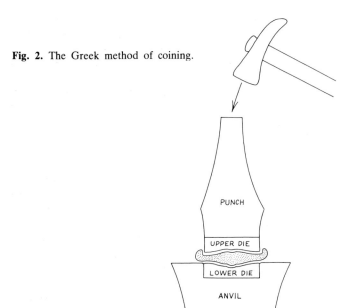

'Attic', was used, in which the principal denomination was the tetradrachm, weighing approximately 17.4 grams. The co-existence of several independent standards obviously caused practical difficulties in the handling and exchange of coins. With a few notable exceptions coins did not travel very far from their home area. But although the difficulties were substantial, they were not insuperable. Moneychangers plied their trade, and there is some evidence for the issue of coins designed partly to assist exchanges between different weight systems.

All the coins illustrated in this book were produced by striking, the procedure being as follows. When metal of the required quality had been prepared, the first task was to create the blanks, or *flans,* of metal, of suitable shape and correct weight. The normal method used to achieve this was casting. The dies were made either from a specially hardened bronze or from iron and were hand-engraved in negative (or *intaglio*), often with remarkable detail. Individual engravers are usually anonymous, though at certain times and in certain places they were in the habit of signing their work. For example, the names are known of several engravers who worked for Sicilian cities in the years around 400 (e.g. Herakleidas, plate 5, number 5; Euainetos, plate 7, number 1). To convert the metal blank into a coin, one of the dies, which was to produce the obverse of the coin, was fixed in an anvil, and the blank was placed on top of it (fig. 2). The other die (which was to produce the reverse), at first a simple punch, later an engraved die, was placed over the blank and was hit with a hammer, so producing the finished coin. No special implements were required for coining, simply the 'anvil and hammer and well made pincers' used by the Homeric goldsmith to gild the horns of a sacrificial heifer (*Odyssey* 3, 434).

The process could, however, go wrong. Too forceful a blow on the upper die might cause the metal of the blank to spread and to well up around the die, and even to split, thus producing a coin of irregular shape. Sometimes either blank or dies might slip, causing a blurring of one or both images. The dies, subject to repeated sharp blows, deteriorated with use; even if they did not break, they could develop minor cracks, which are frequently detectable on the coins they stamped. However, the hand-engraving of the dies and the hand-striking of each coin ensures their individuality as manufactured objects which are often of great charm and beauty.

The types of Greek coins are very varied but can be classified under five main heads. First, many cities chose to honour their patron deities on coins, often in association with objects appropriate to the cult. For example, Hermes is the regular obverse type on coins of Ainos, on the north coast of the Aegean (plate 2, number 1). On the coinage of Elis, in whose territory the Olympic Games took place every four years, the divinities shown were either Zeus, in whose honour the games were held, or Hera, his consort, who also had a temple at Olympia (plate 2, number 2).

A second group of types includes personalities or animals from myths and legends closely associated with a city. Thus coins of Corinth and the cities founded by her frequently depict the winged horse Pegasus, who was believed to have been tamed at Corinth by the hero Bellerophon with the help of Athena; Pegasus, it was said, struck the rock of Acrocorinth with his hoof, thus opening the spring Peirene (plate 2, number 3; note, in the field below Pegasus, a single letter, koppa, the initial letter of the issuing city, Corinth).

Thirdly, local products sometimes figure as coin types. The ear of barley on coins of Metapontion, founded on the coastal plain of southern Italy, recalls the agricultural wealth of the surrounding area in ancient times (plate 2, number 4). The leaf of the *selinon* (wild celery), adopted as the type of Selinous in Sicily, belongs to this class of local product types but shares too some of the character of a fourth group of canting or punning types, where the name of the object shown refers to the name of the city (plate 2, number 5). Such a type was sometimes sufficient to indicate the origin of a coin, as at Selinous, but in other cases appeared with the name of the issuing city, as at Rhodes, where one of the types was usually a rose (Greek: *rhodon*) (plate 2, number 6).

Fifthly, after the death of Alexander the Great in 323, rulers of the various kingdoms that were carved out of his empire began the practice, taken up in the Roman empire and continued in modern times, of placing their portraits on their coins. (Some of these are illustrated and discussed in chapter 6.)

The variety of Greek coin types is not limited to these five categories. Apart from the punch marks mentioned above and the pictorial types illustrated already, an arrangement of letters or a monogram may inform us about the origin of a coin, as well as giving other details such as the name of a magistrate. Thus the reverse of a coin of the Achaean League features the first two Greek letters of Achaea (alpha and chi) in monogram form (plate 2, number 7).

Not all Greek coins were well struck, and not all coin dies were engraved by master craftsmen. But the careful study of a representative selection of Greek coins, ranging widely in time and place, permits direct contact with the Greek world in all its variety of cults and traditions.

Plate 2. COIN TYPES
1. Ainos, silver tetradrachm, early fourth century. Obverse: facing head of Hermes. Hunter 2.
2. Elis, silver stater, mid fourth century. Obverse: head of Hera. Hunter 6.
3. Corinth, silver stater, mid fourth century. Obverse: Pegasus. Hunter 11.
4. Metapontion, silver stater, later sixth century. Obverse: ear of barley. Hunter 3.
5. Selinous, silver didrachm, late sixth century. Obverse: leaf of wild celery. Hunter 1.
6. Rhodes, silver tetradrachm, early fourth century. Reverse: rose. Hunter 2.
7. Achaean League (Mantineia), silver triobol, third century. Reverse: Achaean monogram, with letters and symbol (trident), all within wreath. Hunter 18.

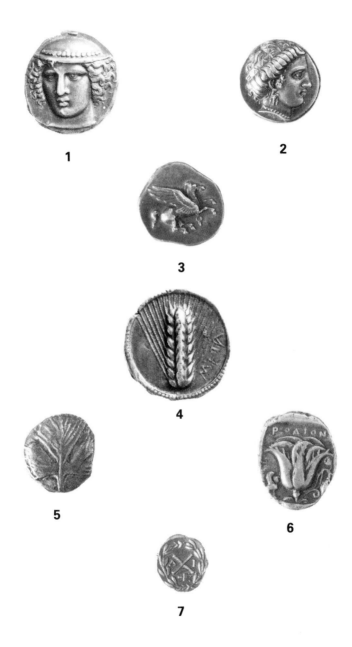

1

2

3

4

5

6

7

4
Coins of the city-states:
south Italy and Sicily

Greek cities in Italy and in Sicily issued some of the most beautiful coins ever struck. They were pioneers, too, in issuing bronze coins on a large scale. Several other peoples shared the western Mediterranean with the Greeks, either immigrants like themselves, such as the Phoenician Carthaginians of north Africa, or residents of longer standing, such as the Etruscans and the Oscan speaking peoples of Italy. In all these areas coins illuminate not only the stories of the Greek settlements but also the relations between Greeks and their neighbours (fig. 3).

In south Italy coinage began in the third quarter of the sixth century, with the remarkable *incuse* issues of several cities on the south coast. On the earliest staters, struck on thin, spread flans, the obverse type appears normally in relief, while on the reverse a closely similar version of the same type is struck in negative, the two types in alignment with each other. Sybaris was one of the cities which used the incuse technique for its coins: the type, of both the staters and smaller denominations, was a bull, accompanied on the obverse by an abbreviated form of the city's name (plate 3, numbers 1 and 2). Sybaris was destroyed in a war with its neighbour Kroton in 510, but it left behind a reputation for luxurious living which has added the word 'sybarite' to our language. Because so little of Sybaris remains above the ground today, the importance of its coins as evidence for its development and prosperity in the later sixth century is enhanced.

At Poseidonia, however, on the west coast of Italy, the early coins complement magnificent architectural remains. The city took its name from Poseidon, god of the sea and of earthquakes, and the obverse of an early coin shows the god advancing to the right, naked except for a cloak draped over both shoulders; his left arm is extended, while with his right he wields a trident (plate 3, number 3). The reverse type is closely similar to the obverse type, and the two fit perfectly back to back, but closer inspection reveals differences of detail, for example in the presentation of the types and in the patterns of the borders. Two closely corresponding but different dies were used. The technique employed to produce this coin was the same as that already illustrated from Sybaris, but the two coins, though both staters of their respective cities, represent different weight standards. The staters of Sybaris, weighing approximately 8 grams, were subdivided into thirds and sixths, while those of Poseidonia, weighing approximately 7.5 grams, were subdivided into two drachms, not three.

Among cities which issued incuse coins was Taras, modern Taranto, founded by colonists from Sparta in the late eighth century. Coinage began here about 500, later than at either Sybaris or Poseidonia, and the period of incuse issues was correspondingly shorter. Thereafter the mint of Taras was continuously active until Hannibal's occupation of the city in the last quarter of the third century, and the coins provide effective illustration and confirmation of Tarentine affairs during three eventful centuries.

The characteristic type of Tarentine coinage was a young male dolphin-rider, either Phalanthos, the leader of the original settlers, or Taras, son of Poseidon, after whom the city was named (plate 3, number 4). On this coin, of a dumpy fabric

Fig. 3. South Italy and Sicily.

characteristic of the immediately post-incuse issues, the dolphin-rider occupies the obverse, while the reverse type, fitting neatly on the flan, is a wheel with four spokes.

Later in the fifth century came the first of a long series of Tarentine coins called 'horsemen', of which the the obverse type is a horse and rider, the horse galloping, cantering or standing still, the rider varying in age, gestures and accoutrements. These types offer remarkable testimony to Tarentine interest in horses and horsemanship. On the obverse of the specimen illustrated (plate 3, number 5), a naked youth rides on horseback to the left, holding a shield and two spears, while the reverse features the dolphin-rider, holding in his right hand a wreath-bearing Victory.

Another notable feature of Tarentine coinage, especially in the later fourth and early third centuries, is the number and frequency of gold issues. These can often be associated with one or other of the succession of foreign generals invited by the Tarentines between 344 and 281 to help them in their numerous wars against their neighbours. The gold stater illustrated (plate 3, number 6) may be associated with the intervention of Kleony-mos, king of Sparta, towards the end of the fourth century. Like all Tarentine gold coins, it was minted on the Attic standard, which was now achieving international status (see further, chapter 6).

The nearest neighbour of Taras along the coast to the west was Metapontion, whose distinctive type, an ear of barley, has already been illustrated (plate 2, number 4). After the incuse phase of the coinage this type was coupled with a long series of heads of divinities and heroes, for example Demeter, goddess of the fruits of the earth, with a wreath of barley in her hair (plate 4, number 1) and Athena, shown in warrior guise, wearing a crested Corinthian helmet (plate 4, number 2). Athena was particularly favoured as a coin type by south Italian cities, for example at Herakleia, established in 433 on a site further along the coast again from Metapontion. Herakleia was a joint foundation of Thourioi (founded with Athenian support in 443, on the site of the destroyed Sybaris) and Taras, and this dual origin is reflected

Plate 3. COINS OF ITALY (1)
1. Sybaris, silver stater, later sixth century. Obverse and reverse: bull turning head. Hunter 2. **2.** Sybaris, silver third-stater, later sixth century. Obverse and reverse: bull turning head. Hunter 4. **3.** Poseidonia, silver stater, later sixth century. Obverse and reverse: Poseidon wielding trident. Hunter 2. **4.** Taras, silver stater, *c* 470-460. Obverse: dolphin-rider. Reverse: wheel. Hunter 1. **5.** Taras, silver stater, 302-281. Obverse: horseman. Reverse: dolphin-rider, waves beneath. Hunter 70. **6.** Taras, gold stater, *c* 300. Obverse: head of Hera. Reverse: young jockey crowned by Nike (Victory). Hunter 21.

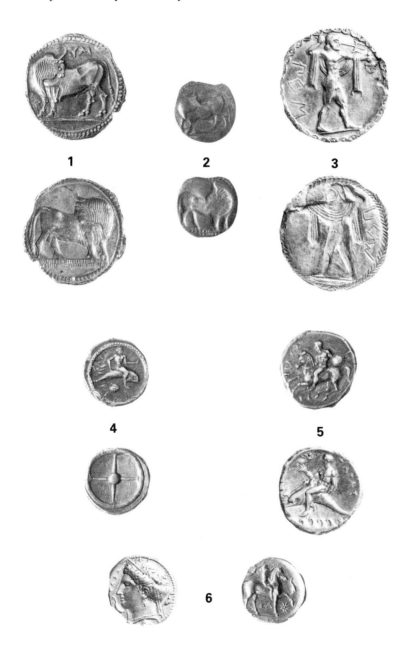

1

2

3

4

5

6

in the types of many of the city's coins (plate 4, number 3). The regular obverse type of its staters was a head of Athena wearing a crested helmet (here the head is facing), while the reverses tended to show the Dorian hero Herakles, after whom the city was named. There is no mistaking him on this coin as, club in hand, he performs one of his twelve labours, the strangling of the Nemean lion.

On the west coast of Italy Athena was a popular choice of type at Elea, founded about 540 by refugees from Phokaia in Asia Minor (plate 4, number 4), and also in Campania, the hinterland of Naples. It was in Campania that Greeks from Euboia first settled in the west in the middle of the eighth century, initially on the island of Ischia (called by them Pithekoussai), then at Kyme on the coast of the mainland opposite. Kyme was the first Campanian city to issue coins, early in the fifth century, and it was soon followed by its daughter city Neapolis (Naples). Both mints adopted Athena as a type at various times during the fifth century and at the beginning of the fourth.

Another group of coins illustrates well the blend of cultures in Campania at that time. The Hyrians were a Samnite people whose coin types are entirely Greek in character: on the obverse a head of Athena, on the reverse a man-faced bull, probably representing a river god (plate 4, number 5). Their name, *Hyrinai,* however, uses an Oscan letterform for R. From approximately the same period, coins of the people of Nola, again with obverse head of Athena and reverse man-faced bull, are entirely Greek in appearance, even down to the alphabet used (plate 4, number 6), but the Nolans for whom they were minted were Italian, not Greek. In the fourth century and later, Neapolis issued coins with some fine female heads on the obverses, in addition to those bearing a head of Athena (plate 4, number 7).

The main reason why Greeks chose Campania for their first settlements in Italy was its proximity to Etruria and its resources,

Plate 4. COINS OF ITALY (2)
1. Metapontion, silver stater, *c* 290-280. Obverse: head of Demeter. Reverse: ear of barley. Hunter 41. **2.** Metapontion, silver stater, *c* 212-207. Obverse: head of Athena. Reverse: ear of barley. Hunter 55. **3.** Herakleia, silver didrachm, early fourth century. Obverse: head of Athena, three-quarters facing. Reverse: Herakles fighting lion. Hunter 8. **4.** Elea, silver didrachm, *c* 400. Obverse: head of Athena. Reverse: lion leaping on stag. Hunter 15. **5.** Hyria, silver didrachm, *c* 400. Obverse: head of Athena. Reverse: man-faced bull. Hunter 14. **6.** Nola, silver didrachm, *c* 400. Obverse: head of Athena. Reverse: man-faced bull. Hunter 6. **7.** Neapolis, silver didrachm, *c* 375. Obverse: head of Parthenope. Reverse: man-faced bull crowned by Nike. Hunter 4. **8.** Populonia, silver 20-unit piece, *c* 225-200. Obverse: Gorgon's head. Reverse: two caducei. Hunter 1.

especially of metals. In return Greek manufactured goods poured into Etruria, along with elements of social and commercial organisation such as the alphabet and the practice of coinage. Etruscan coins sometimes adopt a very rare form in which the reverse is smooth and blank, but the specimen illustrated (plate 4, number 8), from Populonia, on the coast opposite Elba, has the normal two types: on the obverse a Gorgon's head, below which are marks of value (X X, standing for twenty units; one of the letters is off the coin), and on the reverse two caducei placed parallel to each other, but in opposite directions. (The caduceus was a staff carried by the Greek god Hermes; its significance in this Etruscan context is not clear.)

Greeks began to settle in Sicily from about 735, and they built there a civilisation whose monuments still excite the imagination. It was a civilisation of contrasts, in which brilliant advances were achieved against a background of almost continuous warfare and cruelty. As in Italy the Greek settlements were founded from a variety of states in the homeland. There were two main groups, one in the north-eastern part of the island, where towns like Naxos, Zankle (later Messana), Leontinoi and Katane were largely of Euboean origin, and a second group, mainly in the south and west, founded by a variety of Dorian colonists, for example Syracuse (by Corinthians) and Gela (by Rhodians and Cretans).

Naxos marks the natural landfall for travellers approaching Sicily from the southern tip of Italy and was the first Greek foundation in Sicily. It was also among the first to issue coins, in the second half of the sixth century. A specimen of the first series reflects the importance to Naxos of the cultivation of the vine (plate 5, number 1). It features on the obverse a head of the wine god Dionysos with pointed beard and long hair wreathed with ivy. The reverse type reinforces this image: a bunch of grapes hangs from a stalk between two leaves, above the name of the Naxians written from right to left in the genitive case *(Naxion)*.

It was not long before settlers established themselves further

Plate 5. COINS OF SICILY (1)
1. Naxos, silver drachm, *c* 530-510. Obverse: head of Dionysus. Reverse: bunch of grapes hanging from stalk between two leaves. Hunter 1. **2.** Zankle, silver drachm, later sixth century. Obverse: dolphin within sickle-shaped object. Reverse: patterned punch, with shell at centre. Hunter 1. **3.** Messana, silver tetradrachm, mid fifth century. Obverse: light chariot drawn by two mules. Reverse: hare. Hunter 3. **4.** Leontinoi, silver tetradrachm, mid fifth century. Obverse: head of Apollo. Reverse: lion's head. Hunter 11. **5.** Katane, silver tetradrachm, *c* 405. Obverse: facing head of Apollo. Reverse: quadriga. Hunter 11. **6.** Gela, silver tetradrachm, *c* 480-470. Obverse: quadriga. Reverse: forepart of man-faced bull. Hunter 1.

1

2

3

4

5

6

north, on the straits of Messina. Their town on the Sicilian side of the straits was first called Zankle, a name derived from a native word meaning 'sickle', and referring to the curving sandbar which enclosed the harbour of the town. On obverses of early coins of Zankle, in the late sixth century, the curving shape is shown, enclosing a dolphin and the name of the town in the nominative case (plate 5, number 2). The reverse of this coin is created by a patterned punch with a shell at its centre. Early in the fifth century Zankle was ruled first by a body of refugees from Samos, and then by Anaxilas, tyrant of Rhegion, on the Italian side of the straits. He settled the town with Messenians from the Peloponnese and renamed it Messana. Coin types reflect this change and the interests of the man who brought it about (plate 5, number 3): a mid fifth-century obverse shows a chariot drawn by two mules and refers to an Olympic victory in the mule-car race won by Anaxilas, probably in 480; the reverse type, a hare, may refer to the worship of the rustic god Pan.

Several Euboean cities in Sicily chose Apollo as one of their coin types. At Leontinoi, situated in a commanding position on the southern edge of the fertile plain of Catania, a fifth-century coin (plate 5, number 4) shows on the obverse a head of the god, wearing a wreath of laurel, and on the reverse the head of a lion, an animal associated with Apollo, and especially appropriate here as the device of the city (Greek *leon,* a lion). The reverse design incorporates also the name of the Leontines, three barleycorns and a tripod, attribute of Apollo as oracular god. At Katane, towards the end of the fifth century, the engraver of a superb obverse head of Apollo, facing rather than in profile, signed his work — Herakleidas (plate 5, number 5, and cover). The reverse of the coin bears a type popular in Sicily: a victorious quadriga, or four-horse chariot. Observe the galloping horses, the rein of the furthest hanging loose, and Victory hovering above to crown the charioteer.

Among the Dorian foundations of Sicily, Gela began to coin about 490. On the coin illustrated (plate 5, number 6), dating

Plate 6. COINS OF SICILY (2)
1. Akragas, silver tetradrachm, third quarter of fifth century. Obverse: eagle. Reverse: crab. Hunter 15. **2.** Himera, silver didrachm, *c* 483-472. Obverse: cock. Reverse: crab. Hunter 8. **3.** Himera, silver drachm, *c* 500-483. Obverse: cock. Reverse: hen. Hunter 4. **4.** Syracuse, silver tetradrachm, *c* 500-490. Obverse: quadriga. Reverse: small head of Arethusa set in incuse square. Hunter 1. **5.** Syracuse, silver tetradrachm, *c* 485-483. Obverse: quadriga. Reverse: head of Arethusa. Hunter 3. **6.** Syracuse, silver tetradrachm, *c* 465. Obverse and reverse as number 5. Hunter 20. **7.** Syracuse, silver tetradrachm, mid fifth century. Obverse and reverse as number 5. Hunter 23.

1

2

3

4

5

6

7

from about 470, the obverse type is a quadriga, this time with the horses crowned by Victory flying above. The reverse type is the forepart of a man-faced bull, representing the river god Gelas. At Akragas, founded from Gela early in the sixth century, the favoured types were on the obverse an eagle, on the reverse a crab (plate 6, number 1). Between about 483 and 472, the crab appears on the reverse of didrachms of Himera (plate 6, number 2), reflecting a period of domination of Himera by Theron, tyrant of Akragas (a rare example, for this date, of the influence of known historical circumstances on the choice of a coin type). The obverse type of these didrachms is a cock, which had been established as the badge of Himera on the earlier coinage of the city (plate 6, number 3).

At Syracuse coinage began in the late sixth century, and the history of the mint can be traced in detail for several centuries. The earliest coins establish themes which were to dominate the coinage not only of Syracuse but of other Sicilian cities too: a chariot and horses, and a female head. On early coins the head appears within a small circle set in the centre of an incuse square divided into quarters (plate 6, number 4), but it soon expands into a full-sized type, surrounded by four dolphins (plate 6, numbers 5, 6 and 7). This is Arethusa, a local divinity whose freshwater spring can still be seen beside the Great Harbour of Syracuse. It is possible to follow the artistic development of her image over many years. An especially fine representation of Arethusa, her hair bound with a reed, occurs on the reverse of decadrachms issued near the beginning of the fourth century, and signed by the engraver Euainetos (plate 7, number 1). On the obverse of these issues, in the *exergue,* that is the space below the chariot and its galloping horses, a panoply of arms (helmet, shield, cuirass and greaves) is laid out, prizes perhaps for success in the activity depicted above. Syracusan Arethusa types like this one engraved by Euainetos influenced the iconography of many later coin types, including those of Carthaginian coins which were issued in Sicily for military needs, especially the payment of mercenaries (plate 7, number 2). Among the elements of the reverse design of

Plate 7. COINS OF SICILY (3)
1. Syracuse, silver decadrachm, early fourth century. Obverse: quadriga. Reverse: head of Arethusa. Hunter 54. **2.** Siculo-Punic, silver tetradrachm, *c* 320-310. Obverse: head of Arethusa. Reverse: horse's head and palm tree. Hunter 9. **3.** Syracuse, silver litra, *c* 460. Obverse: female head. Reverse: cuttlefish. Hunter 12. **4.** Himera, bronze hemilitron, third quarter of fifth century. Obverse: Gorgon's head. Reverse: six pellets. Hunter 17. **5.** Himera, bronze tetras, third quarter of fifth century. Obverse: Gorgon's head. Reverse: three pellets. Hunter 18.

this coin is a palm tree (Greek *phoinix)* and a Punic inscription signifying 'people of the camp'.

So far attention has been focused on the larger denominations of the coinages mentioned, but many mints issued a range of smaller denominations too. An example from Syracuse has on the obverse a female head and on the reverse a cuttlefish (plate 7, number 3). It is a *litra,* which in Sicily was one fifth of a drachm, a form of subdivision reflecting native rather than Greek tradition. Furthermore, Sicilian cities were among the first to experiment with coinage in bronze, which was issued in various denominations — the silver litra was divided into 12 bronze *onkiai,* or ounces. Examples of a series from Himera show on the obverses a Gorgon's head, on the reverses marks of value: six pellets for a six-ounce piece (or *hemilitron),* three pellets for a three-ounce piece (or *tetras)* (plate 7, numbers 4 and 5 respectively).

5
Coinage in classical Athens

Who issued coins and why? Who used them and how? For most Greek cities there is little evidence apart from the coins themselves to suggest answers to these questions. One exception is Athens, where a long-lasting and complex coinage and the comparative wealth of literary and epigraphic material provide information about the purpose and use of coins. This is especially so in the fifth and fourth centuries, for which historians such as Herodotus, Thucydides and Xenophon provide a detailed framework of events, including from time to time information on financial matters, for example rates of pay or movements of bullion and coins. Speeches delivered in law courts mention details of personal income and expenditure, savings and prices. Among the playwrights, the comedians in particular refer frequently to coins, prices, everyday buying and selling. Public documents erected in stone for permanent display record expenditure on specific projects and sometimes preserve regulations affecting coinage. Some classes of objects, notably vases, were often marked after firing with letters or figures indicating a price. All this material has to be carefully evaluated for possible distortions or exaggerations, and there are big gaps in our information. Taken together however, these sources provide a measure of insight into the monetary affairs of one Greek city.

Athenian coinage began in the middle of the sixth century, but the main lines for future developments were laid down in the last twenty years or so of that century. At that time the silver tetradrachm replaced the didrachm as the standard denomination, and new types were introduced, abandoning the variety of the earliest series, and restricted to a head of Athena on the obverse and an owl (Athena's bird) on the reverse; the origin of the coins was made explicit by the inclusion of the first three letters of the Athenians' name as part of the reverse design. This is the beginning of the famous coinage referred to by Aristophanes in his comedy *Birds* (produced in 414) as 'owls of Laurion', which will 'build nests in purses and hatch little silver pieces'. The 'owls' of Athens are a good example of the way in which coins could be referred to by a characteristic type — compare the 'colts' of Corinth. They were ultimately issued in a wide range of denominations, on a standard known as 'Attic' (table 1 and plate 8), providing a flexible medium of exchange

Table 1. Denominations of silver coins struck at Athens.

	normal weight (grams)	expressed in drachms
decadrachm	43.66	10
tetradrachm	17.44	4
didrachm	8.72	2
drachm	4.36	1
pentobolon	3.63	5/6
tetrobolon	2.90	2/3
triobolon (hemidrachm)	2.18	½
diobolon	1.45	1/3
trihemiobolion	1.09	¼
obolos	0.72	1/6
tritemorion (or tritartemorion)	0.54	1/8
hemiobolion	0.36	1/12
trihemitetartemorion	0.27	1/16
tetartemorion	0.18	1/24
hemitetartemorion	0.09	1/48

100 drachms made up one *mina,* and 6,000 drachms (60 minae) made up one *talent.* Both the mina and the talent were descriptions of weight or value of silver, not actual coins.

which included very small values. However, not all the denominations listed in table 1 were struck together at any one time. Decadrachms for example were issued on only one occasion (in the 460s), and in the later part of the fifth century Athens minted no didrachms and only a restricted number of drachms.

Athenian coinage was overwhelmingly of silver until bronze coins were introduced in the middle of the fourth century. There was an emergency issue of gold coinage in 406, towards the end of the Peloponnesian War; supplies of silver had almost run out, and the gold plates of seven statuettes of Victory were melted down to provide coins ranging from the stater, worth 24 silver drachms, to the hemiobol, worth 1 silver drachm (plate 8, number 10, is a specimen of this issue).

The level of output of Athenian coinage varied with the city's circumstances and needs. Early in the fifth century production of

Plate 8. COINS OF ATHENS (FIFTH CENTURY)
1. Silver tetradrachm. Obverse: head of Athena. Reverse: owl. Oxford. **2.** Silver didrachm. Obverse and reverse as number 1. Oxford. **3.** Silver drachm. Obverse and reverse as number 1. Oxford. **4.** Silver hemidrachm (3 obols). Obverse: head of Athena. Reverse: owl facing, between olive branches. Oxford. **5.** Silver diobol (2 obols). Obverse: head of Athena. Reverse: two owls facing each other, with olive sprig between. Oxford. **6.** Silver trihemiobol (1½ obols). Obverse: head of Athena. Reverse: owl facing. Oxford. **7.** Silver obol. Obverse: head of Athena. Reverse: owl. Oxford. **8.** Silver tritartemorion (¾ obol). Obverse: head of Athena. Reverse: three olive leaves. Oxford. **9.** Silver hemiobol (½ obol). Obverse: head of Athena. Reverse: owl. Oxford. **10.** Gold stater. Obverse: head of Athena. Reverse: owl. British Museum.

1   2   3

4   5   6   7

8   9   10

coins increased enormously, with growing expenditure on a variety of civil and religious construction projects, defence works, and the building and maintenance of a large fleet. Athens possessed its own silver mines, and was ready to exploit them constructively, thus laying the foundations for future successes.

During the occupation of Athens by the Persians under king Xerxes (480) the Athenian mint was closed. When coinage resumed, in 478 at the earliest, it was on a smaller scale than before the Persian invasion, but in the late 450s the production of coins began first to accelerate, then to outstrip earlier levels. The background to this development was the leadership by Athens of the Delian League, formed in 478/7 by cities of the Aegean coasts and islands to guard against future Persian aggression and to recoup some of the losses sustained in the recent invasions. The funds collected on the island of Delos to pay for League expenses (for example, cash payments for naval service) were administered from the start by Athenian officials, the *hellenotamiai,* and in 454 the money itself was transferred to the Athenian acropolis. This move and the further decision, taken perhaps five years later, to spend money contributed by the allies on public building projects in Athens, enabled the Athenians to create a substantial financial reserve, and to pay out large sums from it in the form of coinage.

It is impossible to give meaningful modern equivalents for Athenian monetary values, but some examples of payments and prices can give an idea of the relative scale of expenditure and the relative values of goods that could be purchased.

Military activity was of fundamental importance in the economy of fifth-century Athens, and regular payments were made to those engaged in military service, whether as infantrymen or as rowers in the fleet. During the Peloponnesian War (431-404) the normal rate of pay for Athenian sailors was 3 obols per day, though this rate could be higher if difficulties were expected, for example in the provision of food while on campaign. Figures are available for expenditure on specific operations: for example, 1,200 talents on the suppression of the revolt of Samos (440/39) and 2,000 talents on the siege of Potidaea between summer 432 and winter 430/29.

Payments for state service such as the holding of office were a feature of democratic life in the latter half of the fifth century, and even more so in the fourth. Payment for service on juries was probably introduced in the 450s, and for attendance at council meetings at about the same time. There were six thousand jurymen, and each was paid 2 (3 after 425) obols for every day on which he sat; members of the council received 5 obols a day in the fourth century; payment of 1 obol for attendance at the assembly was introduced soon after the democratic restoration (403); by the late 390s it was 3 obols and later in the fourth century was increased further to 1 or 1½ drachms.

The Periclean building programme in Attica in the fifth century cost over 2,000 talents, and surviving building accounts, for example those of the Parthenon running from 447/6 to 433/2, record expenditure on purchases of materials, monthly salaries (e.g. for architects), daily wages (e.g. to marble-quarry workers, carters and drivers), and payments to sculptors working on the figures of the pediments. The accounts preserved for the building of the Erechtheum between 409/8 and 407/6 show that skilled workmen were paid one drachm (sometimes 1½) per day; the Parthenon accounts suggest that the pediment sculptors, who received a total of 16,392 drachms one year, were not earning much more than this, even though they were doing very skilled work.

These are some of the purposes for which Athens issued coins. Once in circulation, the coins acquired several functions: they were spent by individuals in a variety of ways, or they could be stored as savings. Many items for daily use could be bought for a modest sum: salted fish for an obol each, the same amount for a small measure of wine, for a toy, or for a small oil bottle. Food prices, especially those of cereals, obviously fluctuated, but wheat might reasonably cost 5 drachms per *medimnos* (52 litres), barley 3 drachms per *medimnos*. Items of clothing could be more expensive: up to 20 drachms for a new cloak of good quality, up to 8 drachms for a pair of shoes. Slaves might cost 150 to 200 drachms (more for a slave with special skills), land from 200 to 300 drachms per acre. Thus coinage was used in fifth-century Athens in ways that are recognisable to us today. It was plentiful, it was issued in a wide range of denominations, and it was familiar among all social groups.

6
Coins of the Hellenistic kingdoms

So far, we have been examining a Greek world of independent city-states. In the fourth century, however, this system began to give way, in the eastern Mediterranean to the ambition of king Philip II of Macedon (359-336) and of his son Alexander III (336-323), and in Italy and Sicily before the expanding power of Rome.

At the time of his assassination in 336 Philip II dominated Greece and was poised to invade the Persian empire. This project was carried out by Alexander III, who led his victorious army of Macedonians and Greeks across Asia as far as the Punjab. As a result, elements of Greek culture were introduced to vast areas of western and central Asia, and the political organisation of the Greek world itself was changed drastically and irrevocably. Although the empire left by Alexander on his death in 323 did not long remain a single unit, the individual city-state counted for little in the world of the territorial states carved out of that empire by Alexander's successors (fig. 4). The selection of coins in this chapter illustrates the course and some of the results of these developments, and also introduces some of the personalities who helped to shape events in what we now call the Hellenistic age. The coin portrait is one of the notable achievements of this period. Few portraits of individuals, living or dead, have been recognised on Greek coins before 400, and they are rare too in the fourth century, but after Alexander's death it became usual for rulers to issue coins with a portrait, either of themselves or of a distinguished predecessor such as Alexander or the founder of their own dynasty.

The kingdom of Macedon lay between the Balkans and the Greek peninsula. In classical times its pastoral tribes were ruled by a royal house which claimed descent from the mythical Temenos, of Argos in the Peloponnese. Earlier kings had done much for Macedonia, but it was Philip II who by a combination of organisational and diplomatic skills made his kingdom a power to be reckoned with. An important element in Philip's success was his control and exploitation, after 356, of the gold and silver mines of Mount Pangaion.

Silver coins were issued in a range of denominations, on the standard employed by the Chalcidic League, whose capital, Olynthus, was captured by Philip in 348. Tetradrachms bore on

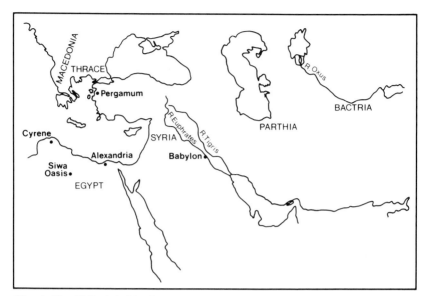

Fig. 4. The Hellenistic kingdoms.

the obverse a magnificent head of Zeus (the first appearance of this god on Macedonian coinage) and on the reverse either a bearded man riding on horseback with right hand raised (possibly representing the king himself) (plate 9, number 1) or a boy jockey carrying a palm of victory (Philip's horse had been successful in the Olympic Games of 356) (plate 9, number 2). Among the smaller denominations, a 4 obol piece combines a similar reverse type with an obverse head of Apollo (plate 9, number 3).

Philip's gold coins were struck on the Attic weight standard. The obverse type of the staters (plate 9, number 4) was a head of Apollo, a type previously used on coins of the Chalcidic League, and now reflecting Philip's close association with the sanctuary of Apollo at Delphi (Philip was elected president of the Pythian games of 346). The reverse type, a biga, or two-horse racing chariot, refers to another of Philip's victories at Olympia. The gold staters were accompanied by smaller denominations, for example, quarter-staters with obverse head of Herakles wearing lion's skin, reverse strung bow and club (Herakles' characteristic weapons) (plate 9, number 5). Herakles, regarded as ancestor of the royal house through Temenos of Argos, had already appeared on Macedonian coins and was to play an important role in the coinage of Alexander the Great. Finally, large numbers of bronze coins supplemented the precious metal coinage: one example shows on its obverse Apollo, on its reverse a horseman (plate 9, number 6); another has Herakles on the obverse, a club on the reverse (plate 9, number 7).

When Alexander crossed to Asia in the spring of 334 his treasury was depleted, but his subsequent conquests, and in particular the capture of Persian treasure, provided ample supplies of bullion for coinage. Many mints were opened, in Asia Minor, the Levant, Egypt and at Babylon, and between them they produced a full range of coins in gold, silver and bronze, of uniform weights and types. On gold coins, Alexander introduced the obverse type of Athena wearing a crested Corinthian helmet, and the reverse type of Nike, goddess of victory, standing with wings outspread, and holding a wreath and an emblem of naval victory (plate 10, number 1). The bulk of the silver coins, now struck like the gold on the Attic standard, were tetradrachms with obverse head of Herakles wearing lion's scalp head-dress, and on the reverse Zeus, seated on a throne and holding an eagle on his right hand (plate 10, number 2). These types are repeated on drachms (plate 10, number 3), and the Herakles type at least on some of the bronze coins (plate 10, number 4).

When Alexander died, his heir (Alexander IV) was not yet born. Subsequently both this boy and a bastard son of Philip II (Philip III) were no more than pawns in the struggle for power which began at once between Alexander's generals. For a time the struggle was for the whole empire, but from 306 onwards several of the contestants assumed the title of king, and by about 270 a world of territorial states had been established, ruled over by descendants of Alexander's generals: the grandson of Antigonus in Macedonia; the son of Seleucus in Syria, Mesopotamia and Iran; the son of Ptolemy in Egypt.

Antigonus Monophthalmus ('one-eyed') had been governor of Phrygia under Alexander. After Alexander's death he determined to bring as much of Alexander's empire as he could under his control (he struck coins with the types of Alexander: plate 10,

Plate 9. COINS OF PHILIP II
1. Silver tetradrachm. Obverse: head of Zeus. Reverse: horseman, right hand raised. Hunter 38. **2.** Silver tetradrachm. Obverse: head of Zeus. Reverse: youthful horse-rider carrying palm. Hunter 64. **3.** Silver tetrobol. Obverse: head of Apollo. Reverse: horseman. Hunter 101. **4.** Gold stater. Obverse: head of Apollo. Reverse: biga. Hunter 2. **5.** Gold quarter-stater. Obverse: head of Herakles. Reverse: strung bow and club. Hunter 35. **6.** Bronze. Obverse: Apollo. Reverse: horseman. Hunter 117. **7.** Bronze. Obverse: Herakles. Reverse: club. Hunter 148.

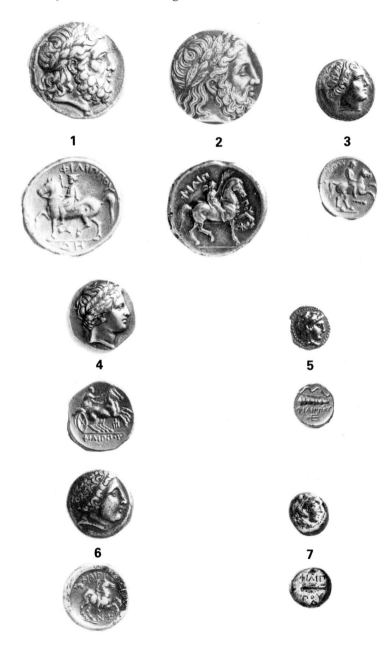

number 5), but he was finally defeated and killed in battle (Ipsus, 301) against a coalition of his rivals. Among these was Lysimachus, who had also been a close associate of Alexander. Starting from his satrapy in Thrace he gradually built up a kingdom which included Macedonia and much of Asia Minor as well, until he too was defeated and killed in battle (Corupedium, 281). It is to Lysimachus that we owe probably the best known coin portrait of Alexander the Great. Anxious to preserve and advertise his links with the conqueror, Lysimachus placed on the obverses of his plentiful tetradrachms a portrait of Alexander with the ram's horn of Zeus Ammon (plate 10, number 6). In 331 Alexander had been acclaimed 'son of Ammon' when he visited the god's shrine at the Siwa oasis in the Libyan desert, and the iconography of his portrait here reflects that of Zeus Ammon, as frequently presented on obverses of coins of Cyrene, in Libya (plate 10, number 7).

Antigonus' son Demetrius distinguished himself in his father's cause, by defeating the forces of their rival Ptolemy in Cyprus (306), and then besieging Rhodes for a year (305/4) — this was the exploit that brought him the nickname Poliorcetes (Besieger). His victory in Cyprus, which was the occasion and justification for the assumption of royal titles by Antigonus and Demetrius, was celebrated on tetradrachms whose obverses show a winged Victory blowing a long trumpet as she alights on the prow of a warship, their reverses showing the sea god Poseidon wielding a trident (plate 11, number 1). Poseidon was Demetrius' patron god, and the closeness of the association is emphasised in another issue of tetradrachms (plate 11, number 2): not only does the reverse show Poseidon, but the portrait of Demetrius on the obverse shows him with a bull's horn, an attribute of Poseidon inviting comparison with the ram's horn of Alexander on coins of Lysimachus.

The death of Demetrius in 283 was followed by a period of changing control in Macedonia before his son Antigonus Gonatas established himself as king over Macedonia and Thessaly

Plate 10. COINS OF ALEXANDER III (1-4), ANTIGONUS I (5) AND LYSIMACHUS (6)
1. Gold stater. Obverse: head of Athena. Reverse: Nike. Hunter 11. **2.** Silver tetradrachm. Obverse: head of Herakles. Reverse: seated Zeus. Hunter 59. **3.** Silver drachm. Obverse: head of Herakles. Reverse: seated Zeus. Hunter 209. **4.** Bronze. Obverse: head of Herakles. Reverse: club, bow and quiver. Hunter 299. **5.** Gold stater. Obverse: head of Athena. Reverse: Nike. Hunter 1. **6.** Silver tetradrachm. Obverse: head of Alexander the Great. Reverse: seated Athena. Hunter 24. **7.** Cyrene, silver didrachm, 308-277. Obverse: head of Zeus Ammon. Reverse: silphium plant. Hunter 34.

(276).He had defeated invading Celts in battle, and his subsequent coinage preserves allusions to the aid received in that battle from the god Pan: for example, a head of the god is shown at the centre of a round Macedonian shield on obverses of tetradrachms (plate 11, number 3). Macedon was the last of the three great kingdoms of the Hellenistic world to settle down to a regular dynastic succession; it was also the first to fall to the Romans. Philip V (221-179) repeatedly came into conflict with Rome; although he suffered a crushing defeat at the battle of Cynoscephalae (197), he continued to build up his resources (plate 11, number 4). His policies were continued by his son Perseus (179-168), but his defeat by the Romans at Pydna (168) brought the Macedonian kingdom to an end (plate 11, number 5).

Seleucus, who had been commander of the hypaspists (a crack guards' regiment), was appointed satrap of Babylon in 321 but did not finally establish his authority there until 312/11. Although he lost his Indian territories, he added north Syria, Mesopotamia, Iran and parts of Asia Minor to his kingdom, which lasted, despite repeated losses of territory, until its remains were conquered by the Romans under Pompey in 63. The Seleucid kingdom embraced many different peoples and cultures, but very little of this variety is reflected in the coinage, which is the product of the Macedonian-Greek ruling minority.

Seleucus began by continuing Alexander's types on his coinage, substituting his own name on reverses after he took the royal title in 305/4 (plate 12, number 1). Around this time, he made a peace treaty with the Indian leader Chandragupta, from whom he received a force of elephants. Elephants were important to the Seleucids and on the reverses of several subsequent issues of coins Athena is shown riding in a chariot drawn by four elephants (plate 12, number 2). The design of this reverse also incorporates an anchor, the personal badge of Seleucus. The chief typological themes of the Seleucid dynasty were established not by Seleucus himself but by his son Antiochus I (281-261): on obverses a portrait of the king, on reverses Apollo, patron of the

Plate 11. COINS OF THE ANTIGONIDS
1. Demetrius Poliorcetes, silver tetradrachm. Obverse: Nike alighting on ship. Reverse: Poseidon wielding trident. Hunter 1. **2.** Demetrius Poliorcetes, silver tetradrachm. Obverse: head of Demetrius, horned. Reverse: Poseidon standing, leaning on trident. Hunter 4. **3.** Antigonus Gonatas, silver tetradrachm. Obverse: shield, with head of Pan at centre. Reverse: Athena Alkidemos hurling thunderbolt. Hunter 3. **4.** Philip V, silver didrachm. Obverse: head of Philip V. Reverse: club within oak wreath. Hunter 3. **5.** Perseus, silver tetradrachm. Obverse: head of Perseus. Reverse: eagle standing on thunderbolt, within oak wreath. Hunter 5.

1

2

3

4

5

dynasty, seated on the omphalos (the 'navel-stone' in the sanctuary of Delphi, regarded as marking the centre of the world), and with attributes such as a bow or a lyre (plate 12, number 3).

In the reign of Antiochus II (261-246) the simultaneous rise of independent kingdoms in Parthia and Bactria began a process of attrition of the Seleucid kingdom which was never subsequently reversed. The Parthians seceded from the Seleucid empire under the leadership of Arsaces, who reigned as king from about 238 to 211 and founded a dynasty which lasted for almost five centuries. The pattern of Parthian coinage was derived from that of the Seleucids (plate 12, number 4): the regular obverse type was a bust of the king; the regular reverse type was Arsaces seated on the omphalos, later on a throne. The legends initially were entirely Greek and in Greek letters: their form began fairly simply, but became more complex with time.

An independent Bactrian kingdom was set up around 250, when a certain Diodotus revolted from the Seleucids. In the absence of narrative sources of information, his coins, and those of subsequent rulers of Bactria, are of outstanding interest both as evidence for the history of the dynasty and as works of art in their own right (plate 12, number 5).

At the western extremity of their realm, in Asia Minor, the Seleucids lost territory to a dynasty based on Pergamum. Philetaerus, son of the Macedonian Attalus, had been put in charge there by Lysimachus, but shortly before the death of Lysimachus in 281 he acknowledged the overlordship of Seleucus I. Tetradrachms issued by him show on the obverse a fine head of Seleucus I, on the reverse, the name of Philetaerus and a seated Athena (plate 13, number 1; compare the reverse type with that on the coin of Lysimachus, plate 10, number 6). Later rulers of the dynasty (Attalus I, 241-197, was the first to take the title of king) all put on their coins the head and name of Philetaerus (plate 13, number 2).

In the face of these secessions Antiochus III ('the Great')

Plate 12. COINS OF SYRIA (1-3), PARTHIA (4) AND BACTRIA (5)
1. Seleucus I, silver tetradrachm. Obverse: head of Herakles. Reverse: seated Zeus. Hunter 6. **2.** Seleucus I, silver tetradrachm. Obverse: head of Zeus. Reverse: Athena standing in chariot drawn by four horned elephants. Hunter 1. **3.** Antiochus I, silver tetradrachm. Obverse: head of Antiochus I. Reverse: Apollo seated on omphalos. Hunter 19. **4.** Mithradates II (*c* 123-88), silver drachm. Obverse: bust of Mithradates II. Reverse: Arsaces seated on throne. Hunter 10. **5.** Heliocles (*c* 150-125), silver tetradrachm. Obverse: head of Heliocles. Reverse: standing Zeus. Hunter Cabinet, ex-Lockett collection (sale catalogue 2752, *SNG* 3362).

1

2

3

4

5

(223-187) tried to restore his kingdom. In the east a large-scale campaign met with some limited successes, but in the west he came into conflict first with Egypt, then with Rome, and by the peace of Apamea (188) lost most of what he still had of Asia Minor. A series of his tetradrachms shows on the obverse a portrait of the king, on the reverse Apollo seated on the omphalos (plate 13, number 3). Antiochus IV Epiphanes, third son of Antiochus III (175-164) attempted to hellenise the Jews (the story is told in 1 Maccabees) and might have achieved the annexation of Egypt, had not Rome intervened. An innovation in his coinage was the addition of elaborate titles to the royal name, illustrated on a tetradrachm with obverse portrait of the king, reverse seated Zeus, holding Nike on his outstretched right hand (plate 13, number 4). The reverse inscription, 'of king Antiochus, god manifest, bearer of victory', proclaims Antiochus' achievements and pretensions: he was successful in war against Egypt and was recognised as a god in his own lifetime. The cult of the ruler was a feature of the Hellenistic monarchies. In Syria, Antiochus III appears to have been the first king to establish a cult of himself in his own lifetime, whereas earlier kings had been content to deify their predecessors. A similar development took place in Egypt, where it continued pharaonic practice.

In the division of responsibilities after Alexander's death, Egypt was given to Ptolemy, son of Lagus, who was related to the royal house of Macedonia. His earliest coins retained many of the characteristics of Alexander's coinage: types, name and weight standard. But it was not long before Egyptian individuality began to assert itself. The obverse type of Herakles (*cf* plate 10, numbers 2-4) was replaced by a portrait of Alexander with the ram's horn of Ammon and wearing an elephant-scalp head-dress and aegis (attribute of Zeus) round his shoulders (plate 14, number 1). Around 315 the reverse type of seated Zeus was replaced by a fighting Athena in an archaic style (plate 14, number 2): Alexander's name remains, but the symbol of an eagle on a thunderbolt seen to the right of Athena anticipates the reverse type of coins struck by Ptolemy in his own name after about 305. Both this type and the portrait of Ptolemy himself on

Plate 13. COINS OF PERGAMUM (1, 2) AND SYRIA (3, 4)
1. Philetaerus, silver tetradrachm. Obverse: head of Seleucus I of Syria. Reverse: seated Athena. Hunter 4. **2.** Eumenes II, silver tetradrachm. Obverse: head of Philetaerus. Reverse: seated Athena. Hunter 9. **3.** Antiochus III, silver tetradrachm. Obverse: head of Antiochus III. Reverse: Apollo seated on omphalos. Hunter 5. **4.** Antiochus IV, silver tetradrachm. Obverse: head of Antiochus IV. Reverse: seated Zeus holding Nike. Hunter 24.

1

2

3

4

the obverse were to persist throughout Ptolemaic coinage (plate
14, number 3). This obverse portrait illustrates well the king's
distinctively craggy features, but he wears too the aegis of Zeus, a
symbol of his divinity. One of his early gold coins has a similar
obverse portrait head, but here the reverse shows Alexander the
Great, wearing the aegis and holding a thunderbolt (attributes of
Zeus), in a chariot drawn by four elephants (plate 14, number 4).
On bronze coins the combination of obverse head of Zeus and
reverse eagle on thunderbolt was to set a pattern for much of the
later Ptolemaic bronze coinage (plate 14, number 5).

   Ptolemy's innovations in his coinage were not confined to the
types. Alone among the successors of Alexander he abandoned
the Attic weight standard and struck coins on a standard lighter
than those used in the other kingdoms (the standard he finally
adopted, often referred to as 'Phoenician', was used at Cyrene).
Whatever the purpose of this change, its effect was to reinforce
the economic isolation of Egypt. Ptolemaic coins are rarely found
outside the lands subject to Ptolemaic rule, unless in association
with specific military or political events: for example coins of
Ptolemy II found in Attica reflect the presence of Ptolemaic
troops there at the time of the Chremonidean War (*c* 267-262).
Within Egypt and certain other areas, such as Cyprus, in the
hands of the Ptolemies from about 295, the coins of the Ptolemies
held a monopoly. Documentary evidence from the reign of
Ptolemy II (283-246) gives an insight into the working of this
policy. A certain Demetrius, probably in charge of the mint at
Alexandria, in a letter to Apollonius, the chief financial official of
Ptolemy II, refers to the regulation by which foreign traders were
compelled to change their money when they came to Egypt,
receiving it back in the form of new Ptolemaic coins. The letter
complains about a disruption in the procedure, on which the
Ptolemies relied heavily for the acquisition of supplies of precious
metals.

   A remarkable feature of Ptolemaic coinage, at least down to
the time of Ptolemy V Epiphanes (204-180), is the number and

Plate 14. COINS OF THE PTOLEMIES (1)
1. Ptolemy I, silver drachm. Obverse: head of Alexander the Great. Reverse: Athena
Promachos. Hunter 1. **2.** Ptolemy I, silver tetradrachm. Obverse: head of Alexander the
Great. Reverse: Athena Promachos. Hunter 5. **3.** Ptolemy I, silver tetradrachm. Obverse:
head of Ptolemy I. Reverse: eagle standing on thunderbolt. Hunter 21. **4.** Ptolemy I, gold
stater. Obverse: head of Ptolemy I. Reverse: Alexander the Great standing in chariot
drawn by four elephants. Hunter 3. **5.** Ptolemy I, bronze. Obverse: head of Zeus.
Reverse: eagle standing on thunderbolt. Hunter 22. **6.** Ptolemy II, gold octodrachm.
Obverse: head of Arsinoe II. Reverse: double cornucopiae. Hunter 11.

1

2

3

4

5

6

quality of gold pieces, frequently with portraits of the kings and members of the royal family. Ptolemy II Philadelphus (283-246) deified both himself and his sister-wife, Arsinoe II, who is portrayed on the obverse of a gold octodrachm with various divine attributes: *stephane* and veil, sceptre (over her left shoulder; its top is seen above her head), and small horn of Ammon. The reverse shows two cornucopiae (horns of plenty) filled with fruits (plate 14, number 6). Portrait heads of no less than four members of the dynasty appear on gold octodrachms from the reign of Ptolemy III Euergetes (246-222) (plate 15, number 1). On the obverse, identified by the inscription 'of brother and sister', are busts of Ptolemy II and Arsinoe II, while on the reverse, with the inscription 'of the gods', are busts of Ptolemy I and of his wife, Berenike I. Ptolemy III himself appears on obverses of octodrachms struck in the reign of his son and successor, Ptolemy IV Philipator (222-204) (plate 15, number 2): his divine attributes include the aegis of Zeus about his shoulders, the rays of Helios, the sun god, and the trident of Poseidon. Philopator appears plain by comparison (plate 15, number 3), while his wife, Arsinoe III, has attributes of divinity, such as the sceptre (plate 15, number 4), already seen in the portrait of Arsinoe II (plate 14, number 6). Their son, Ptolemy V Epiphanes, succeeded to the throne while still a child. The ceremony of his coronation, delayed until 196, was celebrated in the famous trilingual inscription, the Rosetta stone, whose discovery made possible the decipherment of Egyptian hieroglyphs. The youthful portrait of the king reminds us that he died in his twenty-ninth year, of poison (plate 15, number 5). After Ptolemy V portraits of Egyptian rulers become rarer, the coinage in general rather stereotyped. It is all the more remarkable, then, that the coinage of the last and most famous representative of the dynasty, Cleopatra VII (51-30), produces a portrait of outstanding vividness and realism (plate 15, number 6).

Plate 15. COINS OF THE PTOLEMIES (2)
1. Ptolemy III, gold octodrachm. Obverse: busts of Ptolemy II and Arsinoe II. Reverse: busts of Ptolemy I and Berenike I. Hunter, Ptolemy II, 38. **2.** Ptolemy IV, gold octodrachm. Obverse: bust of Ptolemy III. Reverse: cornucopiae. Hunter 25. **3.** Ptolemy IV, gold octodrachm. Obverse: bust of Ptolemy IV. Reverse: eagle standing on thunderbolt. Hunter 27. **4.** Ptolemy IV, gold octodrachm. Obverse: bust of Arsinoe III. Reverse: cornucopiae. Hunter 21. **5.** Ptolemy V, gold octodrachm. Obverse: bust of Ptolemy V. Reverse: eagle standing on thunderbolt. Hunter 19. **6.** Cleopatra VII, bronze. Obverse: bust of Cleopatra VII. Reverse: eagle standing on thunderbolt. Hunter 14.

1

2

3

4

5

6

7
Museums

The following British museums house collections of Greek coins; reference is given to a catalogue or to the relevant volume of the *Sylloge Nummorum Graecorum (SNG)*, where available. Access to the collections may be arranged with the relevant museum department but is normally restricted to those seeking specific information.

Ashmolean Museum (Heberden Coin Room), Beaumont Street, Oxford. Telephone: Oxford (0865) 512651. (*SNG*, volume V.)

British Museum, Great Russell Street, London WC1. Telephone: 01-636 1555/8. (*British Museum Catalogue of Greek Coins*, 29 volumes, various authors.)

Fitzwilliam Museum, Trumpington Street, Cambridge. Telephone: Cambridge (0223) 69501. (*SNG*, volume IV, Leake and General Collections; VI, part 1, Lewis Collection; S. W. Grose, *Catalogue of the McClean Collection of Greek Coins*, 1923.)

Hunterian Museum, The University, Glasgow 12. Telephone: 041-339 8855. (Sir George MacDonald, *Catalogue of Greek Coins in the Hunterian Collection*, 3 volumes, 1899-1905.)

Manchester Museum, The University, Oxford Road, Manchester. Telephone: 061-273 3333.

Marischal College, Broad Street, Aberdeen. (*SNG*, volume 1.)

Royal Scottish Museum, Chambers Street, Edinburgh. Telephone: 031-225 7534. (N. K. Rutter, *A Catalogue of the Ancient Greek Coins in the Collections of the Royal Scottish Museum, Edinburgh*, HMSO, 1979.)

Museums in other countries

Berlin State Museums (Staatliche Museen zu Berlin), Bodestrasse 1-3, 102 Berlin, German Democratic Republic.

Cabinet of Coins (Cabinet des Médailles), Bibliothèque Nationale, 59 rue de Richelieu, 75001 Paris, France.

Museum of Fine Arts, 479 Huntington Avenue, Boston, Massachusetts 02115, USA. (*Catalogue*, A. Baldwin Brett, 1955.)

Museum of the American Numismatic Society, Broadway and 155th Street, New York, New York 10032. (*SNG* volumes.)

Museum of the History of Art: Coin, Medal and Currency Collection (Bundessamlung von Medaillen, Münzen und Geldzeichen), Burgring 5, 1010 Vienna 1, Austria.

National Archaeological Museum (Museo Nazionale), Foro Italico, Piazza del Duomo 14, Syracuse, Sicily, Italy.

National Archaeological Museum (Museo Nazionale), Piazza Museo, Naples, Italy.

National Museum (Nationalmuseet), Frederiksholms Kanal 12, 1220 Copenhagen K, Denmark (*SNG* volumes.)

State Collection of Coins (Staatliche Münzsammlung), Residenzstrasse 1, Munich, German Federal Republic. (*SNG* Deutschland volumes.)

8
Further reading

The only complete handbook of Greek coinage is B. V. Head, *Historia Numorum* (second edition, 1911). C. Seltman, *Greek Coins* (second edition, 1955) was for many years the standard account of the origins and development of coinage in the Greek world. For the archaic and classical periods it is now replaced by C. M. Kraay, *Archaic and Classical Greek Coins* (1976). Excellent surveys of Greek coinage, with fine illustrations, can be found in Max Hirmer and C. M. Kraay, *Greek Coins* (1966; now out of print), and G. K. Jenkins, *Ancient Greek Coins* (1972).

For further discussion and illustration of coinages mentioned in this book see, for chapter 4, G. K. Jenkins, *Coins of Greek Sicily,* British Museum Publications Ltd (second edition 1976); for chapter 5, C. M. Kraay, *Coins of Ancient Athens,* Minerva Numismatic handbooks number 2 (Newcastle upon Tyne, 1968); for chapter 6, M. J. Price, *Coins of the Macedonians* (1974), and Ian Carradice, *Ancient Greek Portrait Coins* (1978), both published by British Museum Publications Ltd. The series of royal portraits on coins of the successors of Alexander are well illustrated (with commentary) in N. Davis and C. M. Kraay, *The Hellenistic Kingdoms: Portrait Coins and History* (1973).

Index of types

References are to the plates not page numbers: e.g. 2.7 refers to plate 2 number 7.

General index